WOKE BABIES®

The Pond in the Park

Written by **Flo Fielding**

Illustrated by **Nathalia Rivera**

DK

Millie's new school was on the other side of town.

"Will we have time to walk through the park today, Dad? And can we zoom through the bee trail and play tip-toe-crow?"

"I think so," said Dad, "and now that spring is here, I've got something special to show you in the park."

As Millie and her dad got to the park gates, it started to rain.

"Who is that waving at you?" asked Dad,
as a car drove past them.

"That's Ivy. She's in my class," said Millie.
"She's nice, but we haven't spoken much yet."

"It'll take time to make new friends," said Dad.
"Some things are worth waiting for, but
you need to wait until the time is right."

"Now... what do we do in
the park on rainy days?"

"Worm spotting!" cried Millie.

"That's right," said Dad. "I bet I can count more worms than you can between here and the pond."

"Not if I count them first!" shouted Millie, as she ran off into the grass.

"14 worms!" crowed Millie.
"I'm the queen of worm counting."

"Would your majesty like to see the special surprise now? It's under this leaf, but be careful near the edge of the pond."

"Is that spotted jelly thing the surprise?" asked Millie.

"It's called frog spawn," said Dad. "Each of those tiny black dots is an egg and in the next few months BIG changes will happen. By the summer, this pond will be full of little happy, hopping frogs!"

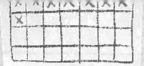

At school that day, Ivy and Millie helped clean up the classroom during playtime, and Millie told Ms. Alfonso all about the pond.

"My Dad said that the frog spawn doesn't turn into frogs right away. It changes into something else first. I wonder what the eggs will turn into..."

"You'll have to wait and see!" Laughed Ms. Alfonso. "Thanks for helping, girls. You can go and play outside now."

"Would you like to go on the climbing frame with me, Ivy?" asked Millie, nervously.

"Sorry, I promised Xander that I'd play soccer with him today," said Ivy, as she ran off.

Whenever they walked to school, Millie and her dad checked the pond. One day something had changed...

"Where have the eggs gone?" asked Millie, confused. "What are those tiny black things swimming in the water?"

"Tadpoles have hatched from the eggs. They have little tails, and gills that help them breathe underwater," said Dad.

"They are so... wriggly!" giggled Millie.

"Yes," laughed Dad. "They have lots more growing to do before they turn into frogs, so they are busy swimming around the pond and getting stronger."

As Millie and her dad left the park, Ivy's car drove past.

"Hi Millie! See you at school!"

A few weeks later, Ms. Alfonso took the class for a nature walk around the park. "Does anyone know what baby frogs are called?" she asked.

"Tadpoles, but they start off as frog spawn first," said Millie, proudly.

"Good job, Millie! You've noticed so much on your walk to school. Look, your tadpoles are changing into froglets now! They still have tails, but they have little legs, too, and they can breathe in and out of the water."

"Okay, everyone, should we see what else
we can find in the park?" said Ms. Alfonso.

The class then went on a nature walk. Ms. Alfonso told
the children about all sorts of different life cycles.

They learned about butterfly chrysalises...

and tree saplings...

and birds' eggs, too!

For the next few months, when Millie was walking through the park with her dad, she shared what she had learned.

"Wow! You know so much about life cycles now," said Dad, smiling.

"Do you think the froglets will be grown up yet, Dad?" asked Millie. "I've been waiting and waiting for so long."

"Come on. Let's go and see,"
said Dad.

But when they got to the pond, the froglets were gone.

"Where are the frogs?"
groaned Millie.

"Maybe they aren't ready yet.
It takes a few months for tadpoles
to change into frogs, but sometimes
they change earlier or later than
that. It's all about getting the
timing right," explained Dad.

You're quiet today," said Ivy. "Are you okay, Millie?"

"I've been waiting and waiting for the froglets to turn into frogs, but now they have all disappeared. Dad says the froglets might not have changed yet," said Millie, sadly.

Ivy thought hard for a moment.

"Or maybe they have changed into frogs, but they're hiding in the park! I can help you look for them after school if you like," said Ivy.

"Really?" said Millie.

"Yes, I have been wanting to see how your froglets have changed ever since our class trip!" replied Ivy.

At the park, Millie showed
Ivy all sorts of things.

"And this is where I zoom like a
bee through the flower beds. Here,
borrow my scooter and you can try it."

"And that old log is where the
crows like to hunt for insects. I play
tip-toe-crow to see how close I can
get to them before they fly away. Ten
steps from the path is my top score."

"This park is so much fun!"
exclaimed Ivy. "And look!
We are at the pond already."

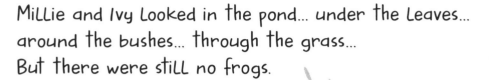

Millie and Ivy looked in the pond... under the leaves...
around the bushes... through the grass...
But there were still no frogs.

Suddenly, it started to rain.

"Quick, under here, girls!" Dad called.
"I think we got our timing wrong for the rain."

"But look!" shouted Millie, excitedly. "We got our timing RIGHT for..."

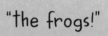

"the frogs!"

Plink!... Donk!... Plonk!

"Mom! There were so many frogs!" said Ivy.

"And we counted 21 worms between the pond and the gate, which is a new queen of worm counting record! It's a lot easier to beat Dad with your help, Ivy," giggled Millie.

"Congratulations, your majesties," said Dad, with a fancy bow.

"Thanks for letting me come frog spotting with you," said Ivy.

"I can't wait to tell Ms. Alfonso about the frogs!" said Millie. "It feels like I've been waiting FOREVER, but all of those frogs were worth waiting for!"

"And I know something else that's worth waiting for," said Dad. "Perhaps your new friend would like to join us for tea? We could have froggy cupcakes."

"Yes, please!" said Millie and Ivy together!

About the illustrator

Nathalia Rivera is a children's book illustrator from the Dominican Republic. She has been drawing and painting since she was young and has gathered inspiration for her work from animals, nature, and various stories. When she's not illustrating, Nathalia spends her time gardening, cooking, and taking naps with her dog, Mimi.

About the author

Flo Fielding is an award-winning, Yorkshire-born writer of dual heritage (Barbadian/English), and a self-confessed "book nerd". Flo writes children's books about identity and family life, and is passionate about children seeing themselves and their families represented in the stories they read. Flo lives in London, England with her husband, two children, and an extremely shy and fluffy cat.

About Woke Babies

Woke Babies is a children's book subscription box service founded by Kelly-Jade Nicholls. Its mission is to awaken and inspire a love of reading in children through the use of diverse and enjoyable literature. It believes that when children are represented positively in stories— heroes, scientists, or simply as the central focus of a great tale—they're given the chance to envision themselves achieving great things. Woke Babies is dedicated to promoting this kind of inclusivity in children's literature and encouraging every child to feel empowered and confident!

Published by Dorling Kindersley Ltd in association with Woke Babies Ltd

Written by Flo Fielding
Illustrated by Nathalia Rivera
Science Consultant Tyus D. Williams

Editor Abi Luscombe
Designer Brandie Tully-Scott
US Senior Editor Shannon Beatty
Senior Art Editor Charlotte Bull
Managing Editor Penny Smith
Jacket Coordinator Elin Woosnam
Production Editor Dragana Puvacic
Senior Production Controller Inderjit Bhullar
Publisher Francesca Young
Art Director Mabel Chan
Managing Director Sarah Larter

First American Edition, 2024
Published in the United States by DK Publishing,
a division of Penguin Random House LLC
1745 Broadway, 20th Floor, New York, NY 10019

A catalog record for this book
is available from the Library of Congress.
ISBN 978-0-7440-9800-6

DK books are available at special discounts when purchased in bulk for sales promotions, premiums, fund-raising, or educational use.
For details, contact: DK Publishing Special Markets,
1745 Broadway, 20th Floor, New York, NY 10019
SpecialSales@dk.com

Printed and bound in China

www.dk.com

This book was made with Forest Stewardship Council™ certified paper – one small step in DK's commitment to a sustainable future. Learn more at www.dk.com/uk/information/sustainability